MANY VOICES
ONE VOICE

Meditations and Prayers
by
Eddie Askew

By the same author:
A Silence and A Shouting
Disguises of Love
No Strange Land
Facing the Storm

©The Leprosy Mission International
80 Windmill Road, Brentford
Middlesex TW8 0QH, UK
1985
3rd Impression 1990

ISBN 0 902731 23 8

Photoset and printed by Stanley L. Hunt (Printers) Ltd, Rushden, Northants

Cover illustration from a pastel painting by the author

Foreword

ENCOURAGEMENT, stimulation and challenge have flowed from the first two volumes of Eddie Askew's meditations and prayers. This latest book is a further collection of thoughts from the monthly newsletters to Leprosy Mission colleagues around the world. The author's prayers and drawings have again been added.

Since 1974 Eddie Askew has been International Director of The Leprosy Mission. Earlier, he and his wife Barbara served the Mission in India.

Santa Maria della Salute – Venice

1 Kings 19:9-13

I'M looking out of my hotel bedroom window in Luxembourg, enjoying the quiet. In a few minutes I must go down to share in a conference. I know many of the eighty people who will be there. Each one comes with his own viewpoint, including me. Some seem very sure of their position; confident in their rightness. Some will be abrasive in debate, others persuasive. A few, even, will be open-minded. Thank God for them. Most will be trying to say something, to convince the rest of us that we should follow them.

So many voices, clamouring for attention. Not only in a conference, but all the time. How do I hear God's voice in it all? The problem is, God doesn't usually shout. He's not strident and aggressive, as many of his followers are! (I grow to distrust Christians who are always so certain of God's will. I'm never sure what insecurities it hides.) He doesn't scream over the shrill noise of opinion and argument. Not for him the insistent hand clutching my arm, nor the body standing in front of me, blocking my escape. He's more likely to stand quietly, and wait patiently until I turn to him. And when he gets through to me it's usually with that "exquisite courtesy" that Mother Julian of Norwich experienced, all of 600 years ago, which leaves me free to choose, or reject.

I still need to hear that voice, though, to recognise it in the clamour, to know with some assurance that it's his. Yet it isn't always clear. Sometimes, when I look to him, I suspect God just smiles at me — still with that gentleness and courtesy — and says "But what do you think? You're grown up, you've got a mind of your own. You decide." It's sometimes frightening, this freedom, but it makes me grow. I make mistakes but, if they're made in good faith and not out of stubbornness or tantrum, he works them into good.

One more thing. I have a strong feeling that it's not as difficult identifying God's voice as we sometimes make out. The problem is that we pretend not to hear it, even to ourselves, because we don't want to do what he asks us to do!

Lord, so much noise, so many words.
Voices, struggling for my mind.
Insistent. Clamorous.
Voices, offering quack cures for old ills.
Trapping me, ensnaring my thoughts
in thickets of uncertainty.

Oceans of opinions, conflicting.
Bottled messages floating on waves of sound,
anonymous, indecipherable.

Words, echoing, reverberating,
bouncing off the walls of my life.
Sliding down in untidy heaps,
to be tripped over
as I stumble to the light.

No time for quiet.

I need help, Lord,
to sort through this jumble of opinion
where everyone is right,
and claims revelation,
world copyright, exclusive.

Sometimes, Lord, I wish you'd shout.
Grab me, shake me, make me listen!
But then you'd be like all the others,
muddied with much talking.
Indistinguishable.

Lord, when I think about it,
how else would you speak
but in a still, small voice?
Your love doesn't compel, or overemphasise.
You wait, in the corners of my consciousness,
with exquisite courtesy, endless patience,
loving gentleness.

But with that courteous, gentle patience
you strip away the pretence,
my self-deluding protest that says I hear no voice.

I hear it, Lord, more often than I want to.
I'm just not ready for what it asks.
Forgive me.

1 Corinthians 13:8-13

A FRIEND showed me some holiday photographs. "That's just what it looked like," he said. It looked great — the sunny beach, the trees, the seaside restaurant — all sunshades and long, cool drinks. I found myself wondering how the local people lived. Was that "just what it looked like" to them? Really, what we should say when we show our photographs is "That's what it looked like to me, at that moment, from that angle".

Photographs are partial. The mere fact that a photo has an edge round it means it's artificial, and that something's been left out. The photographer makes choices and, by a particular viewpoint, or angle, or background, manipulates the truth. He chooses a particular split-second to press the shutter release. What would we have seen if he'd been half a second earlier, or two minutes later? What did he turn his back on, to concentrate on this picture? We know how a picture can be manipulated to allow one figure to dominate, when the truth may have been very different.

We do it without thinking. Travelling overseas we photograph the picturesque, the "unusual" (it's only unusual to us, not to the locals!). We record the bad roads, the worst poverty or, equally misleading, the beautiful. How often do we try for a real balance, filming the ordinary, commonplace life around us?

It's similar with words, with beliefs. We present our strongly-held views as the only possible way of looking at things, and smile patiently at folk who question them. After all, we're right, aren't we? Yet, at best, our views are only partial. Does anyone suggest that the limited focus of our minds can grasp the fulness of God and his purposes? That wise and inspired man, St. Paul, urges us to stand back from our own partial insights, to realise that

> "now we see only puzzling reflections in a mirror"

(1 Corinthians 13:12) or, in the lovely words of the Authorised Version, "through a glass, darkly". The whole truth lies ahead, the moment when everything will become clear, not through a lens, but face to face. For now let's thank God for the insights he's given us, and wait for the fulness that's still to come.

Lord, my problem is I need to be sure.
The puzzling reflections in a mirror worry me.
Throw me off balance.
I'd like everything laid out,
numbered and measured, on a grid.

It would help if I could study the plan,
pin it out on a board, see it all.
I'd like the total picture,
every angle clear and focused.
Analysed, each detailed step, a simple yes or no,
computer-programmed.

Perhaps if I knew more, I'd be less dogmatic.
I seem to shout most when I'm least sure.
It compensates!
But if I had it all, Lord, would I understand it?
Could I cope?
Could I contain it in my mind, my hands?

Lord, if you are love,
and that's the one thing I hang onto
in this raucous, hurting world,
then maybe it's because of love
that you don't show me more.
Just enough to keep me going.
Not enough to overwhelm.

Lord, I'll hold on to the love.
Not the knowledge. My mind's not up to it.
And anyway
even Paul seems less than sure about knowledge!
One minute he says it will vanish,
the next that it will be whole.
So in the confusion — mine, Lord, mine — not yours,
I'll settle for love.
Always there. Available.
Poured out and overflowing.

And really, Lord,
it's not important that I should know,
but that you know me.
And if I'm sure of that, and sure of love,
then, surely,
I can take the rest
on trust.

Matthew 11:2-6

I'VE been thinking about John Baptist; reading about him too, in the first chapter of John's Gospel. What a masterpiece it is. Those first verses are tremendous. Tight, concise writing. Profound truth distilled into short, simple phrases. Every word hitting the target. Nothing wasted. That's how to communicate!

But back to the other John, the Baptist. We are told he was "sent from God . . . as a witness" (John 1:6). He was privileged to introduce Jesus, and baptise him. John was the herald. John prepared the way. Then he was jailed and beheaded. John never saw the fulfilment of his work. His ascetic life in the harsh sun and cold winds of the desert hills, his moments of joy in identifying the Christ, abruptly ended. John saw neither the cross nor the resurrection. He helped with the painting, but never saw the finished picture. He's there for a moment, playing his own vital part in God's plans, and then the action moves on, out of his experience. Other people take over, events developing in ways John could never have expected.

That's life. We plan and work, making our contribution the best we know how. We try to shape things in the way nearest to what we believe is God's will. Not seeing clearly beyond the next decision, but trusting him to work things out. That's the key word — trusting. Being prepared to commit ourselves to his direction, doing all we can to stay sensitive and responsive, but leaving the end result with him.

The fulfilment for us may not lie in seeing the end in our beginning, but in doing our own little bit with all the faithfulness we can bring to it. After all, it's God's plan, not ours. And we know that he'll be there at the end, just as he was in the beginning. We know too that, if what we are doing is within his will, it will be accomplished, whether we see it to fruition, or not. That thought can take a lot of the frustration out of our work, and help us put it in perspective. We are part of the continuing processes of the Kingdom of God, beginning before us, going on beyond us, yet surrounding us and carrying us along, in love.

Lord, I feel for John.
It must have been tough.
He was used to a hard life,
but that was in the sun and the wind.
Not in a prison cell.
No sweet-smelling violets there!

But worse,
the powerful memories. Of you.

And now, the painful questions.
Doubts.
His own identity at stake.

"Are you the Messiah?"

Or was it wasted time?
One brief flame of hope
burning his fingers.
Leaving ashes, drifting, on the wind.
Ending painfully.
I know you were close to him, then.
As ever. Standing near.
I hope he knew it.

Lord, I'm grateful
that I, too, have a place
in your design.
I have to admit
I hope it won't end
like John!
But it's good to be involved.
Committed.
And when it all falls into place
it feels great.

Sometimes, though, it isn't easy
to see where I fit in.
I feel I'm working in a vacuum.
Nothing connects.

I can't see my place in your plans.
Lord, your purposes go way beyond my horizon.
I can only look back to yesterday.
I can only see ahead to tomorrow,
and that not clearly.
Eternity's a bit big for me,
I've not grown to fit it, yet.

Lord, when I'm puzzled,
uncertain,
help me remember
you're in control.
Your finger on the button.
And, whether I can see the end or not,
help me accept
that you know where we're going.

Lesotho Plains

Psalm 95:1-7

ILOVE painting skies. They vary so much — sunny and clear, or misty, skies heavy with dark raincloud. So much subtle colour — warm and cold greys, shapes insubstantial yet solid. There's the sudden burst of sunlight as clouds part, bringing the landscape dramatically to life.

Painting is about light. The interplay of light and dark, the contrasts, the way each bit depends on every other bit. The way one colour modifies the colour next to it. It can be breathtaking to work on a painting, to build it up and then, with a few considered or, more often, fortunate brush strokes of high key colour, to see it spark into life. A tiny bit of creation really. It doesn't happen very often! But there are times when the strokes of colour don't produce that feeling of light. Then you look at the painting in dismay until you realise that the problem is a lack of contrast. The shadows aren't deep enough. The light tones don't register because the darks aren't there. The brilliance of the one depends on the depth of the other. And the feeling of light is produced by deepening the darks!

Even further, if you look closely at a landscape painted by a master, you'll see that in his lights there are subtle hints of the shadow colours; and to bring real unity and harmony the light colours have to be there in the deep shadows, enriching them. It's not a case of either dark or light, but of both. And you begin to realise that the darkness and shade in a landscape are an indication, not of the absence of light, but of its presence.

The interplay of pattern, of light and dark, is always changing. It's part of the joy and frustration of painting. A never-ending exploration. You struggle to get to grips with a particular composition, and then the clouds increase, and the light changes. The clouds roll on, the sun shines. Never ending, endlessly varied, yet the changes are grounded on concrete things, on the warm earth, its contours, its solidity. The light may change in a moment, but the shape of the hills will still be there, tomorrow. A moment's change may bring out different colours but the form of the hills, their structure, is still there, the same. Dependable.

Shadows and light, continually forming and reforming, dissolving, reshaping across the landscape of my life. It's unsettling, joyous, frightening, frustrating, stimulating. Yet beneath it, in it, reassuring and strengthening, the hand of God.

Painting it with love.

Lord, sometimes
I'm attacked by hope.
It creeps up on me.
Unawares.
I'm in the middle of a problem,
finding it hard to see the way ahead.
Shadows, one after the other,
nearly blotting out the light.
Clouds, charging across the field of my vision
like panzer divisions.
And almost, Lord,
almost, I enjoy the misery.
The brief and petty martyrdom.
The picture won't come right.
I'm ready to give up,
throw the whole thing away.
Why bother?

And then, Lord, the hope.
Hard to see, difficult to grasp.
Quiet. Undefined.
A feeling for the ground I'm standing on.
The strength of the hills.
Yours.
The deep places of the earth.
In your hands.
Strong hands, warm, enduring.
And I see, dimly
in your perspective
the light and shadow.
Not in conflict,
but each with a place
in the total picture of my life.

And when it's complete, exhibited,
Lord, no one will ever know
how I struggled with it.
They'll just look.
"Don't like that," they'll say,
or "That's nice". And move on.
But you and I, Lord, we know.
And all I need is your smile
and a nod to say you understand.
And then, perhaps I will!

1 John 4:17-19

T *RAVELLING In*, by Monica Furlong, is a wise book. I found it on the "remainder" shelf of a local bookshop. Is that this world's judgment on wisdom, or the world judging itself? At one point in the book Monica suggests the need to "renounce perfection for wholeness". That startled me!

Renounce perfection? "Do I have any perfection to renounce?" I wondered. Then my mind's eye saw the sort of person we call a perfectionist: someone who tries obsessively to do every job, large or small, without the slightest fault. So important does it become, that the job is done and done again, polished and repolished — and never quite finished. A lifestyle that leads to anxiety and frustration.

But doesn't the Bible talk about people "of perfect heart"? Doesn't Jesus himself encourage his disciples to be perfect, as in Matthew 5:48? And if the Bible says it. . . ? Yes, but what does the Bible actually mean? Beware arrogance at this point. We Christians are very fond of dressing up our opinions as God's truth and covering up our insecurity in dogmatism. Even so, I've been looking at what the word seems to mean in its various contexts. Briefly the Old Testament seems to use "perfection" in the sense of integrity and loyalty to the Lord. The New Testament usage implies maturity and completeness. What I've *not* found — put me right if I'm wrong — is the way we use the word with its intense "perfectionist" implications; living every detail of life faultlessly. This seems to me to have little to do with wholeness. It's more like a disguised striving to earn God's approval, to justify ourselves.

Wholeness lies in looking at ourselves, with all faults, and accepting what we see, in love, because that's what God does. Then we can spend our energies, not in striving for "perfection" but in developing our relationships, with the Lord and with each other. "What is devilish about perfection," writes Monica, "is that it always seems attainable and it never is." And while we're tensely and painfully reaching for it we remain unbalanced and hypercritical. That's far from the wholeness of life in Christ. The clearsighted but loving acceptance of ourselves doesn't mean we stop trying for better things, but it does mean we can stop tearing ourselves — and others — to pieces with the destructiveness of criticism and daily guilt, and the agonising over every detail of failure. In a small book of poetry by schoolchildren, a fourteen-year-old girl writes of wanting "to be accepted as me: an original with no form of copy". It means we can stop looking at ourselves, and others, and start looking at Jesus. That's where wholeness lies.

There are moments, Lord,
when I'm dazzled by the wonder of it.
Forgiveness.
It's hard to take in.
Not only that your love
can crystallize itself into forgiveness.
But that you can find time
for me.
That my feelings and my life
awaken your concern.
And that in love, in Jesus Christ,
you can accept me,
welcome me into your Kingdom.
With all faults.

And yet, Lord,
in my self-centred consciousness
my failures overshadow me.
Guilt lurks in the dark corners of my mind,
claws flexed, eyes bright,
ready to pounce,
give lie to love's reality.
My pride fights on
in protest at love's gift.

Lord, let me absorb the truth.
No need to struggle,
fight to earn parole.
No need to make excuses, or explain.
Your love embraces me.
The rest is cancelled.

For me, simply to hold
in joy and tremulous certainty
this one great revelation.
That only in accepting
both forgiveness and myself
am I made whole.

1 Corinthians 13:1-8

SIMON WESTON was twenty years old when he was terribly burnt during the Falklands Campaign. He was a soldier waiting to disembark from a ship when it was incinerated by an enemy missile. Many of Simon's mates died. He survived, but only just. I watched an intimate and very moving TV programme about his later progress through hospital. His face is very badly scarred, and, even after skilled plastic surgery, very disfigured. His hands and fingers are severely disabled.

The first thing that came through on the screen was the wonderful resilience of the human spirit. During his months in hospital and subsequent rehabilitation there were times of depression and times when he screamed with pain. Mostly, though, one saw Simon's courage, his matter-of-fact acceptance of what had happened to him, and his strong determination to fight back to life.

But the most moving experience was to listen to his mother talking to him. Gentle, but persistent, just chatting about home, food, birthdays, she brought him stability and simple encouragement. And it was brimful with love. She saw the scarred face, the burnt body, but it was so apparent that she was looking through that, to the real person underneath, her son. Whatever had changed, his identity hadn't. She knew the real Simon, and loved him. That's the strength of human love, made in the image of God's.

"I will send peace ... as a river," says the Lord, "... as a mother comforts her son, so will I myself comfort you" (Isaiah 66:12-13).

Life scars us, we shout in pain and anger, we scarcely look "made in God's image", yet he loves us. He sees beneath the surface to the real person, so much in need of comfort, strength and healing. And no matter what we look like, we are accepted.

The question of war and its justification is a different one. I'll risk only one comment: nationalism looks a dangerous basis for life, when you see what it did to Simon.

Lord, can I just concentrate on your love, today?
So often, when I talk with you,
I concentrate on me.
My feelings. My bruises.
I come to you breathless,
agitated from fighting all the ills
— real and imaginary —
which people my world.

My world, Lord ? Sorry, your world.
A world you built in love. For love.
And though at times it seems out of balance,
like the wheelwobble of an old car,
you built it in love.
Made it for love.

I thank you Lord, for all the evidence I see.
Not in abstract debate or routine sermon,
three points, every Sunday,
six feet above my head,
but love at work.
Love in the tender eye, warm hand stretched out.
The empathy and sweet sorrow of shared pain,
as one stands by another.

I see the beauty of your love.
Honeylight warming the stony ground around me.
The generous breeze of love,
blowing in every corner,
lifting the dull dust of routine
to make life sparkle once again.
Polishing the worn corners of my life
until they glow.

And love's particularity I see.
Making me one with you.
Not as some segment of computer database,
but just as me.
Made in your image.
Cared for. Treasured. Unique.
And, Lord, I see the cost of love to you.
No easy option, bought with small change.

But sacrifice, free-given.
The cost was life, for life.
From you to me.
I take it, Lord, your life, your love,
and hold it to myself.

I'll live in it today.
And pass it on.

Severn Estuary Farm, England

Isaiah 11:1-9

I SAW a fascinating news report. Koko, a gorilla weighing more than three hundred pounds, had taken a kitten as a pet. It happened in California. Shortly after Koko was born, a psychologist took over her upbringing, and began to teach her a sign language developed for the deaf. Over twelve years Koko has learnt, and uses, more than five hundred words and signs. Some time ago, she signed that she wanted a kitten — she'd been shown pictures of them. The psychologist gave her a woolly toy kitten. Koko rejected it and asked for a real one. I have some lovely photographs of the result — this great gorilla cradling her tiny pet with great tenderness.

Some years ago I visited Lambarene, the hospital created by Albert Schweitzer, in Gabon. There I befriended a baby gorilla, an orphan of about three months, its mother having been shot by a hunter. I've never known an animal so in need of affection. We would sometimes play together, but more often it would just cling to me, holding tight. There were problems! At only three months it weighed about forty pounds, and it could cling with hands *and* feet. It was difficult to disengage!

The behaviour of these two animals set me thinking. Misunderstood as savage, dangerous animals, "all they need is love" to paraphrase a song by the Beatles. Part of the problem is that we stereotype both animals and people. We latch on to one characteristic and overemphasise it. "Foxes are cunning" we say, "Lions are fierce." With humans we classify a whole nationality as noisy, arrogant, or mean. We do it with individuals too. We say a co-worker is uncooperative or difficult. We close our minds and look no further. We believe our own prejudices and never try to change things.

Now here is Koko, a gorilla, quietly breaking our assumptions. Learning a language, communicating, and showing elements of tenderness. How different from the stereotype. Maybe, dare I suggest it, we should apply this insight to the "gorillas" we work or live with! If we dropped our prejudices maybe we'd find tenderness in them too, under the surface.

Perhaps there's a weakness in my argument. Koko was born in a zoo. Maybe you could argue that she's not normal, she's never had to face the threat of harsh life in the forest. True, but she still has her instincts — they can't be bred out in one generation, a few years. So maybe there's another thought here: if human beings could be brought up in an environment where threats and violence were not accepted as a part of common life, maybe they'd grow up loving, too!

Lord God, Creator,
all life is yours.
All that has come to be
has come through you.
Lives in your energy,
takes breath because you willed it.
Is clothed in your beauty,
your dignity.
Part of your world.
Valued and loved.

Lord, I too am a creator.
My shallow judgment
creates deep prejudice.
My lazy assumptions
conceive misunderstanding.
My lack of love
brings misery to birth.

Teach me, Lord,
to love what you have created.
Help me to shed the arrogance that cocoons me
and restricts my growth.
Help me to split the binding threads
and crawl out into the warmth of your light.
Stretch the wings of my understanding.

Teach me to see people
one by one.
Not to pigeonhole them, categorise.
Not to hammer them into unnatural moulds
of my own making.
But to rejoice in every difference.
To accept people as they are.
Each one a part of your creation.
Showing something of your glory.

At times, Lord,
I meet people
I can see no good in.
No glory.
No redeeming feature.
Lord, is that true?

Or is it just my eyes?

1 John 4:19-21

TO see ourselves as others see us can be helpful, when we've got over the salutary shock. A Muslim, living in England and writing in my daily newspaper, criticises Christians for their arrogance and the way in which, for example, medical missions "take advantage of sick people by making them a target for their evangelism when they are at their weakest and most vulnerable". Don't rush into self justification for a moment, there's a lot we could say in reply, but just think about it. That's the way some people see us. That's what our motives look like to some eyes. Unfair? I hope so, I believe so, but it's good to be sensitive to what others think — not to the point of being frightened to act because of it — but to check on our motives and behaviour.

"Well, you can't please everybody. You'll be criticised whatever you do." Yes, I know, but there's a bit more to it than that. Looking through a book of prayers — *Hear Me, Lord* by Michael Walker — I was struck by a phrase: ". . . the power of service, the temptation to place others in our debt by what we do for them out of interested love". Now of course we are "interested" in the people we serve, not only in their physical needs but in their personalities and souls as well. Our help and concern though are not crowbars to prise open unwilling yet vulnerable minds, but sincere demonstrations of God's love and power, showing in concrete terms what we are saying in our words. But we need to be aware of the danger to our own integrity, of engineering gratitude for favours done, of expecting a response, and then of being dissatisfied when there is none.

We need to be "disinterested" in our love in the sense that we love people for their own sakes, and because Christ did, and that we don't use our love or service to manipulate them. There are possessive parents who wreck their children's lives out of "love", but it's a love of self and not of the child. People must be free to make their own response and we must respect their right to do so, as Jesus did. Their transaction is between them and God, and that's the relationship which we are working to encourage, rather than a dependency on ourselves.

I'm trying to get it straight, Lord,
but it's not easy sorting out my motives,
the reasons why.

The problem is, Lord, that in this world,
the only one I've got for now,
something for nothing doesn't fit.
Price tags on everything.
Free samples through my letter box
only to encourage me to buy.
I give in order to receive.

I keep, in some dark corner of my mind,
a passbook record of each investment,
expect return from love's transactions.
With interest. At 10.5 percent.
Date stamped. Tax-paid.

My love makes obligation.
Tries to buy response.
I'd like to be a king,
with grateful courtiers hanging on my every move.
Word-perfect in obedience.

Can love demand?
Lord, in the quiet, you come to me, gently.
Showing your love in bleeding body,
broken for me,
but leaving me, with quiet courtesy, to make my move.
No pressure, argument. No blackmail.
Just arms held wide, self-giving.
No preconditions. No sense of obligation.

Teach me to love like that.
To give and not to count the cost,
and not to seek reward or gain.
Help me to understand
that love is a wild bird,
born only in freedom. Flourishing uncaged.
Help me rejoice
when I can help another into free flight,
and send him soaring
into the wind of your Spirit.
Reward enough.

Luke 10:38-42

THIS isn't the first time I've quoted Carlo Carretto, one of the Little Brothers of Jesus. In his *Letters from the Desert* he records a shattering encounter with the Lord. "Come with me into the desert," says Jesus. "It is not your deeds I want; I want your prayer and love."

My immediate reaction was mixed. Most of us are busy doing things; what would happen to our work or our patients if we weren't? And, anyway, doesn't Jesus show the importance of practical caring for others in that picture of people sharing the Kingdom because "... when I was hungry you fed me ... clothed me ..."? (Matthew 25:35).

Let's take a cool look at it. I don't think for a minute that what we do isn't important, and I don't believe the Lord does either. Our work isn't being discounted, but sometimes we hide behind what we do. We put up our work as a smokescreen to hide the threadbare reality of what we are underneath. We hide from ourselves. We'd rather not know. And we use our work, too, to shield us from the God we profess to love. *The Choice*, a book on the contemplative life by an Anglican nun, Sister Kirsty, suggests something very similar — that we fill our lives with activity to avoid facing what God really wants of us. (Incidentally, it's a very honest book and has given me a more open understanding of that kind of vocation.)

I find it helpful to put the Matthew chapter alongside Jesus' searching examination of Peter in John 21. "Do you love me, Peter? Do you love me?" Questions painful as a knife wound, cutting deep. Jesus leading Peter to face what he really was, not what he would have liked to be. The Lord wanted Peter's love, not just his protestations or his work, and Peter needed to see that there was no substitute. It can hurt to strip away the activities and face what is left, and yet we need to do it. We need, sometimes, to "disengage" and make sure that our personalities rest on Christ, and not on work, however praiseworthy the work is. That's one reason why some folk find retirement hard to take — without the work role there's nothing left.

More than once I've faced lovely, humble Christians who've said, "I wish I could have done what you've done for the Mission. I've done nothing but pray." When the Lord makes his assessment, I wonder how he'll rate that? We could be in for a few surprises.

Lord, love can hurt!
I feel the pain which Peter felt
as he heard your question.

Do you love me?
But, Lord, you know it. You can see it.
Here I am giving time, now, to reading and prayer.
Everyday. Well, whenever I can.
Sorry about yesterday, there was just so much to do.

It seems unfair of you to ask, Lord.
Of course I love you.
Look at all the work I do.
So busy, running hot with righteous sweat,
as I dash from one commitment to the next.

And still you ask.
Lord, what do you want?
I plan and work, and organise.
My spiritual chequebook stubs can prove it all.
I give my time, my mind, my energy.
And in the evening, home at last,
collapsing in my easy chair,
I know I've done a lot for you.
I can't do more to prove I'm yours.

My love?
But it's all there, Lord,
I'm trying to show you. . . .

Lord, help me make a quiet place, a space
where you and I can meet at peace.
Where I can sit and wait, and listen.
A calm where loving eyes can meet and interlock.
Not frantic in haste,
a brief handwave from passing cars.
But in the slow contentment of two friends together.
Maybe no need even to speak the words
I love you.
You know I love you.
Because I give you time.

And then, Lord, when I plunge back into the busyness
it looks different.
Because I don't need it to prove I love you.
And I can do it with the joy
that comes from having been
with you.

Mark 4:35-41

MOTHER Julian of Norwich was a hermit, living in 14th century England. Her life of prayer was anchored in the reality and love of Jesus. Not totally isolated, as we often imagine earlier Christian mystics, although her lifestyle and priorities were meditation and prayer. It's a much harder role than we activists realise. It was a harsh world of suffering and inequality. Yet she could look through and beyond it to the ultimate goodness which surrounded her in the small stone room in which she lived, and proclaim with certainty, "But all shall be well and all shall be well and all manner of thing shall be well".

Her faith was nothing superficial, like the froth in a beer glass, but a deep affirmation that the world is moving to its ultimate rendezvous with love, and that the journey itself is made in love. Sometimes hidden or disguised, yet there for the discerning heart to know, here and now.

And there is always something more to find. Isaac Newton, the 18th century scientist who formulated the law of gravity after the apple fell on his head (a better use of apples than Eve's), realised this. "I do not know what I may appear to the world," he wrote later, "but to myself I seem to have been only a boy, playing on the seashore, and diverting myself in now and then finding a smoother pebble, whilst the great ocean of truth lay all undiscovered before me."

It's the sense of pilgrimage. We move on, easily or painfully, through an ever changing pattern of discovery, a pilgrimage simultaneously in two worlds — the world of the world, and the inner world of ourselves and our relationships — which are really one world, the world God made, and moving to the consummation God wills.

All shall be well, Lord?
It's hard to grasp in this struggling world.
Earth's foundations eroding,
stained dark by seas of suffering.
Evil surging, waves crashing with destructive force
on moving sand.
Threatening cliff-falls of faith.
Lashing the puny breakwaters of belief,
threatening inundation.

Yet, all shall be well?
Seasick with seasonal anxiety,
the hard knot of panic just below my heart,
I look to you.
Wondering. Doubting.
Is your hand stretched out yet again?
Will you restrain the storm,
bring peace?

Lord, you are the still centre of every storm.
In you is calm,
whatever the wind outside.
In you is reassurance,
however high the waves.
In you is strength,
however contrary the tide.

I put myself in your hand.
The sea is vast. No landmarks.
I don't know the way.
At times I can't even point to north.
Or where the sun sets, hidden by cloud.
But I'm content to leave the navigation to you.
To meet the unknown.
To find, if not new continents of faith,
at least an island or two.
Knowing that, in spite of storm strength,
all shall be well.

And Lord, there are other sailors,
other ships.
I pray for them, today.

Matthew 9:9-13

L EADING the "Free Israel" campaign more than 3,000 years ago, Moses believed passionately that his people were meant to be free. It was God's will. (Moses was sometimes reluctant to head the campaign, but that's different!) He also believed, logically, that if Pharaoh and his advisers were opposing the movement they were opposing God's will. So when the Israelites successfully completed their escape over the sea, Moses naturally celebrates with a victory song. "God has triumphed...." Read Exodus 14 and 15. Very human and understandable, but was it perhaps a bit regrettable? Reading it through again, I wish the song had been a bit more restrained and thoughtful, although I don't know any patriotic victory songs which are restrained. You see, the Egyptians were God's people too! Because we habitually think of the Israelites as "chosen people" we tend to forget God's concern for the rest.

God loved the Egyptians as much as he loved the Israelites. "There is no distinction between Jew and Greek" (Romans 10:12) wrote Paul, many years later. The context refers to equality within the faith, but it implies, surely, God's loving concern for all people. God doesn't have favourites — although the way some of us pray for our countries you'd think he had. God's deliverance was cause for praise and joy for Moses but what of the drowned Egyptian soldiers, just doing what they had been told to do? What of their grieving families at home? I'm getting on to tricky ground, but while I'm sure God willed freedom for the Israelites, I'm equally sure he didn't want to bring suffering and death to the Egyptians. Moses may have rejoiced at what he called God's war-like nature, but I don't believe it pleased God to see people die. Here's a case, if ever there was one, for looking at the Old Testament with New Testament eyes. If God is love now, then he was love 3,000 years ago!

By opposing his will the Egyptians brought down on themselves inevitable and tragic destruction, but although Moses found satisfaction in it, I don't believe God did. Remember 1 Corinthians 13 — love is never glad when others go wrong. A coin has two sides — my "success" may be built on another's failure, my wellbeing on another's suffering — and whenever I'm proved "right" I need to remember that the loser is as much a child of God as I am, and just as precious.

And don't forget that when I categorise him or her a sinner, that puts him straight into the class of people for whom Christ died — in love!

Lord, it's so convenient to divide your world
into us and them. Goodies and baddies.
The ones you love and the ones you don't.
Clear compartments. Classified.
And as long as I'm on the right side
— and I always am, Lord,
because I'm the one who classifies —
there's a nice feeling of satisfaction.
Superiority.
And when others go wrong,
I can always be relied on, if not to comfort,
at least to point out clearly to them where they went wrong.
Just trying to help!

Lord, forgive me that sideways glance,
the wry smile that marks another's failure.
Protect me from the milli-second judgment
that makes folk guilty with computer-speed.
And just as thoughtlessly.
The readiness with which I write them off.
Unserviceable.

Widen my blinkered vision, to see your love at work
beyond the comfortable scope of my complacency.
And help me recognise the possibility
that just occasionally I may be wrong.
Help me to find the honesty
at least to whisper my confession,
if not to say it loud.
Let me feel your arms
not just round me in privileged security
but open wide in welcome to the world.
Not easy, Lord.
Even in church I hate to move along my pew
to make a space for others.
It's easier to suggest they sit elsewhere.
Protect me from the thought
that, somehow, your love belongs to me,
and that I need to be consulted in its use.
Help me to recognise it's yours
to share with all, including me.
And, Lord, on those occasions
when I do seem right,
help me to tread with gentleness.

Psalm 46

THIRD Class Ticket, a book by Heather Wood, describes the experiences and reactions of a group of Bengali villagers on a weeks-long tour of India. It was financed from the will of an old lady, Uma Sen, who wished her tenants to see the wonders and diversity of their own country. It's a fascinating study of how they coped with the stress of the new and unknown. They hold together for protection as they walk the crowded, concrete streets of Calcutta, struggle with technology as they visit a factory, react to food cooked by strange hands. It's neither a patronising nor a clinical book, but an acute, warm-hearted record of what one person observed and shared.

At one point an old grizzled farmer, his mind racing to absorb and deal with what he is experiencing, says: "We have seen so much these days. I feel I would know India better if I had my hands upon a plough." There's a whole world perspective in the words. On one level it's a cry for the security of the familiar. Change can be frightening, battering our senses as we seek to adjust to it and change ourselves. We all need a stable framework in which to live and grow, and we often underestimate the effects the threat of change has on people. Why do you get such a negative response to a new idea, or a new method of working? Why is it so hard to change community attitudes? The threat is real and change has to be slowed to a rate at which people can adjust to it.

Deeper down, the farmer says that there's a need to relate change to what we know and to what makes us feel anchored. New experience must relate to present experience or the computer in our heads rejects it. Imagine Stone Age man's reaction to the U.S. Space Shuttle. It would be so far out of experience as to be incomprehensible. And until our new knowledge is integrated with the experience we already have it stays peripheral, useless. If travel enriches us by widening our understanding then it's good, but it doesn't always. I've observed world travellers coming back with vision as blinkered as when they left. As one cynic has said: "Travel narrows the mind". It may not be their fault; folk can be just too insecure to cope with the demands of new experience.

On the deepest level, I believe the farmer is asking for the strength of something enduring and what, in human terms, is more enduring than the plough? Not the bits of wood and iron, but what it suggests — the land, the seasons, the process endlessly repeated of seed, fruit, harvest. Can we call Christ the plough? The enduring and eternal word of God, the security on which I stand, the familiar strength which I grasp as I face change and stress; the assurance that though "heaven and earth shall pass away, my words will never pass away" (Matthew 24:35). The one to whom I can relate my new experiences, and in whom I can assess and evaluate them. And with his stability I can cope with the rest.

Lord, my mind races.
A blur of images, impressions
moving too fast to think about.
Words, pictures, happenings crowd in, insistently.
Rioting in my mind, uncontrolled.
Hurling rocks to shatter my security.
I feel under attack.
Nothing is what it seems.
Nothing is what it was.
And what it will be, I have no idea.
Changing, all the time.
It shakes me, Lord.
The minute I've taken in this one new thought,
feel comfortable with a new process,
there's yet another treading down my heels,
pushing hard to get by.

I need you, Lord.
A safe refuge. A shelter.
I used to scorn that thought.
Shelters were for the weak, and I was strong.
But pride's not what it was,
that's changed too,
and who am I, when mountains shake
to stand out in the storm?
I head for cover with the rest.
Cold with shock.
Another of the walking wounded in the fight.
I need your reassurance.
The strength that comes from you.
Yet even you, Lord,
come to me in different ways.
Speaking new words in unexpected moments.
Shaking what little complacency I have left.

And Lord, when I take a break,
gasping for breath
at the end of this day's lap,
I realise you never promised things would always be the same.
Rebirth means change.
Walking with you is transformation.
Uncomfortable. Painful at times.
Filled with newness.
New life, and joy, and love.
Help me to cope with it.

Because you promised,
and I think I've got it right,
your hand in mine.
Calm strength flowing through to me.
From you. The unchanging one.

Small Schooner, Indonesia

1 John 4:7-12

I'M feeling very humble at the moment. My ego makes sure it doesn't happen very often, so I must make the most of it!

I've been exchanging letters with the mother of a mentally handicapped baby. The mother's been reading one of my books, *Disguises of Love*, and she wrote questioning a suggestion I made that we must be careful about assuming that particular tragedies were God's will. She said I'd taken her anchor away: that in the nineteen months since the difficult birth which had left her daughter handicapped, she'd found the strength to cope by believing that God had willed her baby to be born that way, and that he had a purpose for her life.

I wrote back, undogmatically, agreeing that God must have *allowed* it, but suggesting that that was very different from saying that he'd *caused* it. I said I couldn't believe that the Lord deliberately willed the handicap, any more than I can believe that he wills the deaths of thousands of children by famine in Africa, for example. The important thing, I suggested, was not the question, or its answer, but the way God strengthens us to meet our problems, and how he begins to work with us to create good out of them.

She wrote again, very honestly and thoughtfully. She could now understand that "the Lord allowed me that crutch to see me through a very hard time, but I realise I can't be an effective Christian on crutches. Your book," she wrote, "has taken away the crutch, and I'm stronger for it."

Hallelujah! She needed no strengthening from me, the Lord was already working at it with her. She's already responding with "something beautiful for God", as Mother Teresa would say, in surrounding her daughter with love. "Really, I don't see her as a handicapped child, but as a special child who creates a lot of love," she writes. "There will be a lot of problems, I know, but God will create a blessing for every hardship."

One day, I'd like to meet that family. I'd like to meet them at Christmas, as they surround their baby with love. I wonder — maybe I'd see a star over the house, hear an angel singing "Glory to God in the highest . . .". No shepherds — just an occasional visitor like me, gazing in wonder at love incarnate in, and through, a handicapped baby. And aren't we all handicapped, in one way or another? It's just that with most of us our handicaps aren't quite so obvious.

Lord, we'd have done it differently,
your coming to earth.
Press Releases.
Banner headlines.
Discussion on telly.
All the hype of the supermarket.
We'd really have sold it, Lord.
Your coming.

Yet you chose to come as a baby.
Helpless, dependent.
To a carpenter and his wife.
No better than she should be,
I expect they said.
Away from home,
on the road.
Not the sort of people we'd notice,
except to joke about their accent.

And yet your arrival
moved the world.
Shook it. Changed it.
Shone light in dark places.
Brought hope and love.
Especially love, Lord.
Not the pale reflection we show,
but love as a flame.
Burning into our lives,
bright, clean, pure.
And burning itself out
on a cross.

And yet, in the burning out,
lighting new flames.
Flames of faith and hope.
Spreading warmth across the world.
Love, rich in a poor stable.
Love, discounted on a cross.
Glorious in resurrection.
Tangible in human lives
made beautiful, today.

Lord, help me reach out
to touch it.

Luke 9:57-62

AN East German Christian leader recently described the life he and his fellow-believers led in what he called "Churches in Socialism". "We spent our earlier days wishing we were elsewhere, wishing that conditions were different," he said. "Then we gradually came to understand, and accept, that we are where God has put us, and that this is where he wants us. Our job is to live and witness to his love and salvation here and now." Great words, courageous words, from the Communist world.

When the going gets tough, we all want to change things. Many of us are free to make changes. We can change where we live, the work we do, even our friends. We can resign, move on to other things. Perhaps we do it too often. Sometimes it's the Lord's will. Sometimes that's just what we call it! Billy Graham says, "We carry our conscience around in a wheelbarrow, pushing it in the direction we want it to go". Isn't there a point in staying where we are when things get difficult, to show that it's possible, and that endurance counts for something?

Sister Kirsty writes in *The Choice*, "It is not the place where you are that is the important thing. It is the intensity of your presence there. It is not the situation that counts. What counts is that you are fully alive in any situation . . . looking hard at the place where you are, instead of wanting to work wonders elsewhere."

I suppose Jesus, in the stable at birth, or on the cross at death, might have wished he were elsewhere. Yet he was just where God wanted him, right where God could use him to the full. With us the dilemma is that we don't always have the comfort of knowing it at the time. In Graham Greene's novel *Monsignor Quixote* — a little jewel of a book — a companion says, "Time will show", but Quixote answers, "Time can never show. Our lives are far too short." We do sometimes have the comfort of a clear conviction that we're doing the right thing, but not always. God's time is different from ours. When life is hard we hang on by faith, not proof. What's that you said? "It's easy for you, sitting at a desk in London"? No, it's no easier here than elsewhere. There are times for all of us when anywhere else seems better than here and now.

"Three times I begged the Lord to rid me of it," confesses Paul (2 Corinthians 12:9), but the answer was: "My grace is all you need". Is that all, Lord?

Lord, it's good being part of your kingdom.
Belonging. In the community.
I can relate who I am and what I do,
to you.

Sometimes, though, it wears thin.
The ceaseless sandpaper friction of life
rubs through the thin veneer
I thought so solid.
The scratches score deep and hard.
I don't like it that way.
When I said I'd follow you,
I meant it, Lord,
but I didn't know it would be like this.
There are times when I want out.
I thought the cross was his, not mine.
And when its shadow falls across my shoulders
I feel the weight.
Just the shadow, Lord!
I want to twist and turn
and slide it to the ground.

And yet, when I look a little further,
deeper,
I see your hands,
not white and manicured
but scarred and scratched and competent,
reach out
not always to remove the weight I carry
but to shift its balance, ease it,
make it bearable.

Lord, if this is where you want me
I'm content.
No, not quite true. I wish it were.
All I can say, in honesty is this.
If this is where I'm meant to be
I'll stay. And try.
Just let me feel your hands.

And, Lord, for all who hurt today,
hurt more than me,
I ask for strength,
and that flicker of light,
the warmth, that says you're there.

Luke 22:39-46

I NEVER *Promised You a Rose Garden*, a novel by Hannah Green, tells of the struggle of a teenage girl to come to terms with her schizophrenia, and to find the strength to cope with the strains of life outside the hospital.

"Look here," says her psychiatrist, "I never promised you a rose garden. I never promised you perfect justice . . . and I never promised you peace and happiness. My help is so that you can be free to fight for all of these things. The only reality I offer is challenge, and being well is being free to accept it or not at whatever level you are capable. I never promise lies, and the rose garden world of perfection is a lie . . . and a bore, too!"

One can almost hear Jesus saying words like that as he calls us to commitment and discipleship. It's so easy to start with our problems and yearn for a world where everything's fine, and nothing ever goes wrong. Some Christians seem to think that's the way it ought to be, peace given to us on a plate, but it's a phantasy world, and phantasies are dangerous to live in! There's no escape from reality — no healthy escape anyway — and to remain whole means facing up to life as it is.

The Christian way *does* offer peace and happiness, but not the phantasy sort, and not divorced from the stresses of life in the real world. Jesus offers a challenge; a challenge to sit loose to our fears and anxieties and to reach for freedom — not freedom from stress, but a freedom to struggle for the things that are worthwhile. And peace has a dynamic quality — *shalom* — where stresses and relationships are held in balance and harmony, the basis of that harmony being our relationship to God. That's what makes life good, and expands human personality — yours and mine. The rose garden world of perfection, here and now, is a phantasy, but we can begin to share in the life of the Kingdom which Jesus has established and which will, in the fulness of his purposes, become the only reality.

I like a garden, Lord.
Not the hard work. Digging, cutting.
Weeding, pruning.
I'd rather leave that to others.
But a place where I can relax.
Smell the flowers,
heavy scented on still air.
Watch the play of light on bright colour.
Dig fingers into cool grass
from the soft shade of protecting trees.

And under it all,
the strong purposes of life,
cell on cell, building,
growing in ceaseless rhythm,
taking your sustenance as birthright.
An ordered world, calling for prayer, for quiet praise.

You had a garden, Lord,
Gethsemane.
No roses there,
unless you count the sweat,
like clots of blood, rich red.
Thorns in abundance,
soon to be round your head,
pricking with sharp anguish.
Small daggers of derision. Rejection.
And soon the tree, new cut,
sap weeping for shame,
holding your body.
The chemistry of pain
fertilizing the ground of suffering.

Stony ground, Lord.
And yet you raised a rich crop.
From tears sprang joy.
From blood new life.
Seeds of hope,
grown in love and sacrifice,
germinate in hope.
From weakness,
strength to overcome the world.

Lord, help me move out
from my garden of quiet indulgence
to live in the real world.

Help me to challenge,
meet life as it comes.
Anew. In your power, your love.
Help me rejoice
in the freedom of your presence.

Mungrisdale, Lake District

John 1:1-14

SOMEONE'S given me a new toy. It's a pocket calculator. So what's new about a calculator? Well, this one is solar powered. It has no conventional battery which needs replacing when it runs down. It has a small solar cell which converts light falling on it into electrical energy. As long as there's enough light to see by — natural or artificial — the calculator works.

I've always understood that light is illumination; the opposite of darkness. If there's no light, I can't see, and I fall over anything in my path. But light does, in fact, do more than illuminate. A green plant goes yellow and sickly in a dark room. Light's necessary for health. It can also change chemistry. That's what photography is based on. Light goes through a lens, and so changes the chemicals on a piece of film that an image can be created and kept.

Today, though, I see a further dimension in my experience of light — light as a source of energy and power. Through the solar cell, if it's big enough, people gain the electrical power to run radio transmitters, refrigerators, and other machines.

When Jesus claims to be "the light of the world" we understand, quite rightly, that he was talking about illumination — holding up the truth for us to see, helping us understand things better, dispelling darkness as we walk along the road. But, however much we probe, there are always new dimensions to God's truth. The "light of the world" is also a source of energy, *the* source of energy. He was "with God at the beginning, and through him all things came to be". He is the power of creation and the energy that keeps the cosmos whirling.

And John says that "to all who did receive him . . . he gave the right to become children of God" (John 1:12). Some translators write: "He gave the *power* to become . . .", so Jesus not only shows the way, he gives the power to walk it. Christians have long accepted that as a "spiritual" truth but, through my calculator, I now see the natural world backing it up!

The other interesting thing is that if I put my hand over the cell so that it's in shadow the calculator doesn't work. Now there's a thought!

Lord, I turn a stone in the garden
and little creatures scuttle from the light.
Content to live in shadow.

Lord, light of the world,
There are times when your truth
seems too big for me.
Too bright.
The light shines in my eyes
and on my ego.
Shows clearly what I really am.
So clear that even I can see it!

I shrink, and turn for shadow.
You ask so much.
To live in light so bright
that every movement, every thought, is known.
Seen. Understood.
That's hard,
until I realise that the light
flows freely from a flame of love.
Not cold and dead moon-glow
but warm and living sun.
Light, not simply to reveal my nakedness
but clothing me in love.
Light showing me the way.
Not as a dim candle
in some small cottage window of my dreams,
far hope, with nothing for the road,
but bringing in its glow
the power to live.

Light, taut,
crackling with creation power.
Whirling with the energy
that shows not just the way
but gives the strength to make the move.

And, glory be, it has a name.
Your name.
I don't worship light or power,
but love. Called Jesus.
Lord keep me in his light.
And when I creep towards the shadows
roll the stone away, once more.

Ephesians 2:11-22

MARTIN LUTHER KING led black Americans in the civil rights movement of the Sixties. He was a great orator. Once heard, his words echo through the mind, each echo getting louder, not softer. "I have a dream," he affirmed. A dream of a time when people of all races will live together in peace. "I have a dream ... of a time when people will be accepted for the content of their character and not the colour of their skin."

He was killed for his dream. Killed, because the dream challenged the way things were, and began to change things. It could have been a harmless dream, just words. Nice sentiments. And Luther King might have lived to a soft old age. The trouble was he believed that his dream could become reality. This gave him, and his followers, the courage, and what courage it was, to face the hysterical hatred and blind violence of people who were frightened by the dream.

His dream and his courage were important, but to me the greatest thing about him was that, while he was prepared to die for his dream, he wasn't prepared to kill for it. Idealism is so easily corrupted. People are coerced "for their own good". Today's world has many killers who are deformed idealists, who will not only die for their beliefs, but also kill. That's where things go wrong.

The Christmas revelation to the shepherds at Bethlehem links "peace on earth" with "goodwill to all people", and both are preceded by "glory to God" (Luke 2:14). Goodwill, not violence, brings peace and glory to God. Threatening "the other side" with destruction produces, at best, a stalemate where no-one gets killed, but let's not call it peace. There was no weapon in the gifts the wise men brought to Jesus! And later, when Jesus said: "I have come not to bring peace, but a sword," he was facing people with the fact that his "dream" would be so unacceptable to some that they would resist it violently. He was not using the sword as a threat.

Peace can only come when people are prepared to die for their ideals, but not to kill for them. Michel Quoist makes a similar point, and says: "only then will people have laid the foundation for peace". I'm not quite with him there though. Christ has already laid the foundation for peace. Our job is to build on it.

Lord, it's so easy to sound off.
Shout and scream at the world as it is.
So easy to pick out the violent men.
To hold them responsible for all that's wrong.
So easy, in the armour of self-righteousness,
to take up their weapons.
Meet force with force.
So easy to fall feet first
into the trap of hate and prejudice,
and find I'm caught between its iron jaws.
Held tight.
My feelings violent as theirs.
Hooked and high on hate.
Sweating it out for my next fix.
Anger addictive as heroin.

Lord, give me the strength
to hold fast to love.
Hold fast to you.
I see you, hanging on the cross.
"Father, forgive them . . ."
But sometimes, Lord,
they **do** know what they do!

And still I need to love.
If violence defeated violence
then violence would be left. Victor.
Lord, the victor must be love.
Was love, on the cross.
To death and beyond.
And on the third day,
in your resurrection life
I find the courage to begin.
Tremulous, hesitant as a new-born lamb,
I stand with you, in love.
Staggering and uncoordinated,
yet the hope is there.
That as I live in you
and you in me
the love will grow.
The dream become reality.

Acts 17:16-34

IT'S a great thrill to walk through Athens and visit places St. Paul knew. There's the Acropolis, a commanding hill, still crowned by the great remains of the Parthenon. Below it, to the north, lies the Agora, the ancient market place, still linked by the worn stones of the Panathenic Way. Here Paul walked and saw the altars and images, and here in the market square he cleared his throat of the dry dust and began to speak about his God. The area is impressive, even today. How much more so for a First Century Jew? High marble buildings, carvings painted and gilded, thronged with people. The centre of art, culture, philosophy. Paul was educated, a Pharisee soaked in Jewish learning, but I imagine that many of those sophisticated, worldly Athenians saw him as a country bumpkin. He spoke fluent Greek but "My dear, wherever did he get that accent? A bit rural, isn't it?"

Yet Paul faced them, beginning where they were, arguing clearly and forcefully and, later, continuing the debate on the Areopagus, the still-bare, craggy hillside to the west of the Acropolis. To the walkers of the Panathenic Way, the processional road up to the temple of Athene, he made known his knowledge of The Way. Not with great immediate success apparently. There were a few converts — Dionysius and some others — but we have no Epistle to the Athenian Church in the New Testament.

There's another hill, Lykkabetos, in the heart of modern Athens. At the top is a tiny, white walled church. To one side a bronze tablet records, in Greek and English, words from the Revelation of John (15:4): "Great and marvellous are thy deeds O Lord God, sovereign over all; just and true are thy ways, thou king of all the ages."

In my reading of it, I emphasised the pronoun "thy", the God whom Paul preached. Looking back from the hill towards the Acropolis one sees that ancient Athens is dead. Its stone skeleton, lying warm in the sun, is still visited by compulsive, camera-clicking tourists like me. Masons chip away, replacing worn marble with new. (Actually "new" marble is just as old as the "old" marble when you think about it — it's just quarried later! It's only the carving that's new.) But the power has gone. Athene, Artemis, Zeus; the gods are dead. Yet the faith Paul preached in its vulnerability, the blossoming of love, is alive and well. Philosophies have crumbled, their strength vitiated, but love goes on. Not in great stone edifices, but through lives lived in Christ. I noticed little flowers growing in crevices between the stones. Their offspring will still be there when the stones are dust. Such is the persistence of love. Individuals may be trampled on, but love springs up, ever new. And will continue to do so.

It must have been hard to believe, Lord,
in ancient Athens.
Hard to believe that the future
lay with Paul.
Standing there, small, in the market,
trading words and ideas.
Words on the wind,
caught in passing
on the antennae of butterfly minds.
Handled in brief listening
and dropped.
Rejected.

Vulnerable words.
A vulnerable god.
No golden image, shining in a temple.
God in blood on a cross.
Bruised, aching.

Words of love.
Unrecognised, irrelevant.
Of little value at the stalls.
Love, kicked into a corner
by unconcern.
Lying with the rubbish.

Yet persistent.
Growing quietly in the crevices,
blossoming in suffering.
Seeding itself in human lives.
Penetrating the stone.
Quietly.
Building a kingdom,
not in cool marble
but in human lives,
made new in hope.
Made new in Jesus.
Eternally new.
Indestructible.

Lord, take the cold stone
of my world
and warm it
in the sunlight of your love.

Judges 6:33-40

I'VE just been rereading the story of Gideon in the Book of Judges. The Israelite farming community was being harassed by hordes of Bedouin nomads — the Midianites and Amalekites — swarming in from the desert. The Israelites were hiding in the hills. Gideon is driven to think through his faith. He rebels against the religious conventions of his day and then, prompted by God, sends out a call for action. The usual translations say: "The Spirit of the Lord took possession of Gideon" (Judges 6:34 NEB) or: "The Spirit . . . came upon Gideon" (AV), but a marginal comment suggests that the verb literally meant "clothed". So "The Spirit . . . clothed himself in Gideon" (my version). That seemed to say something to me.

The impression of the usual translations is of God as an irresistible force taking over Gideon, leaving him no choice, railroading him into a course of action whatever Gideon thought about it. I don't believe God works that way. The Spirit stirs our conscience, or persists in holding a challenge in front of our eyes, but the decisions are ours. The Spirit clothes himself in us, inhabits us, and in sheer gracious humility works through our personalities allowing us the initiative. The "takeover" idea is intellectually easy and can be used comfortably to hide our mistakes. How often have I heard someone say "That's what God wanted at the time", when a little more honesty to oneself might have prompted "I made a mistake, I'm sorry". It's so easy to pass the buck to God and imply that his guidance is responsible for the error!

That can't be true. God doesn't turn us into machines, but he clothes himself in us, his love respecting our freedom to be what we are. It's a liberating thought: that in Christ my personality is free to develop and not just to toe a party line. But the responsibility is firmly with me too! In clothing himself in me, God depends on me. My behaviour must allow the Spirit freedom to express himself through me. People look at our clothes and judge the person within. The world looks at us — as the Spirit's clothes — and reacts accordingly. It's an enormous adventure to be freed from the chains which stunt our development, and to be given the strength and courage to live for him. And, at the same time, to know that I can hold on to my personality without being moulded into a fixed pattern. It's not an excuse for irresponsibly doing your own thing because, remember, the Spirit clothes himself in us and is therefore hidden or revealed by what we are and do. But we can still be ourselves, and maybe we can even find the grace to allow others to be themselves — even the ones we live with, or work with!

The wonder of it, Lord.
I'm not just a puppet, strings attached,
dancing to your moods.
Some see the world like that,
a dreary ballet, cosmic choreography,
purpose dim and indecipherable.
But in the light you give
I see your graciousness.
Sending your spirit, not in coercive power,
but gently.
Fitting its form, freely, to my life.
I welcome you.

I feel the joy.
That I can go through life, just as myself.
No crippling mould of mass-production.
No two alike.
Custom-built. One-off. Myself.
Nowhere near perfection,
but loved, as me.
No need to fight to be like someone else.
Blessed with your liberty, free-given.

But, Lord, my freedom lives only in you.
In sharing life with you.
I could so easily put back the chains you've broken.
Resell myself to slavery.
Guard me, Lord,
from misusing, in your liberty,
the gifts you've given.

Give me the strength to live for you.
That folk may see your life through mine.
Your love in me.
Your hand stretched out through mine.
Your purposes fulfilled in all I do.

Psalm 121
Hebrews 12:1-2

OVER the years I've almost submerged myself in books and find it difficult to get rid of a book I've enjoyed reading. Beyond the reading I'm also interested in the development of books, from early clay tablets to papyrus, from scrolls to the form of book we know today, and all that's gone into its production — design, print, illustration and binding. Among my books is a collection of a hundred or so which I treasure greatly. They represent the development of book production over the last 500 years and include some old and beautiful leather bindings. Apart from a small piece of Egyptian papyrus, 1800 years old, the oldest I have is a single page of a 14th Century illuminated manuscript of Psalm 121. I value this, and some later Bibles and Prayer Books. Among them is an 18th Century Book of Common Prayer which I discovered on the shelves of a bookshop, and which my wife's sharp eyes recognised through its Armorial binding as being something special. It was. A bit of research showed that it came from St. George's Chapel, Windsor Castle.

Besides the fact that they have survived so long, what fascinates me about these old books, particularly the Christian ones, is the thought of who has owned and read them, gained help, insight and comfort from them. I wonder who wrote out that manuscript of Psalm 121, five hundred years ago, and said "Amen" as he read the promise: ". . . The Lord is your guardian. . . ."?

Another Bible I have, dated 1696, belonged to a Dr. Stukeley, who became an Anglican minister in 1729. It's full of his written notes and comments, in Latin, Hebrew, Greek and English.

People long dead, their lives and culture very different from ours, yet reading and believing the same words, basing their lives on the same faith in the same Lord, sharing in the life and worship of the organic community which is the continuing Body of Christ. I find it encouraging to catch this vision of the great company of Christian people — "the great cloud of witnesses" — of whom we're a part. A long, historic tradition, truth enduring and strong, yet new to each generation, speaking afresh to us, and continuing to meet our needs as it met the needs of people of earlier days.

Depressed, discouraged, unsure of where your roots are? The faith is enduring, not only in the physical survival of old books, but in its infectious transmission from individual to individual. And we are part of it.

Lord, sometimes I feel alone.
Vulnerable.
Standing in a wasteland.
I see nothing ahead, nothing behind.
Just one hard-edged moment of tension.
I freeze.

And then I see, behind, around me, people.
Women and men who've lived their lives
in the faith I hold.
Who've lived, and died,
in the wonder of your love.

If I could meet them now, in flesh,
medieval mystic, scribe,
illiterate workman,
Renaissance priest,
we'd span great gulfs,
seem strangers from another world.
I'd want to say the classic words:
"Take me to your leader."
And when they did
I'd find their lives
based on the same mystery of your love.
Their hopes, their fears bound up in you.
Same Lord. Over the centuries.
Which should be no surprise to me,
seeing that you don't change.
The same forever. The unbroken thread
reeled out for lifeline
as I walk, warily, sometimes wearily,
through the confusing maze of dark and light
that is my world.
The thread goes back to you.
Goes on to you in the uncertain future.
Uncertain only in my own brief view
tentative beyond the next horizon.
But sure in you.
In the strong chain of lives lived,
deaths died,
in your hand.

Lord, it's good to know
that I, too, am part of your purposes.
Seen, known. Acknowledged.

Treasured, not for my own perfection or performance,
But for myself.
Part of the mystery, the great unfolding,
little by little,
of your Kingdom.
Lord, bring it soon.

Morning Mist, Bhutan

Matthew 16:21-28

I HAVE a crucifix on my office wall. I hesitated before I put it there. Many Christians find a crucifix helpful, but others don't. Many Christians prefer the symbolism of an empty cross, reminding us that Jesus not only died but is alive again. Some would rather not use any form of cross at all. So why the crucifix?

For nearly 250 years, until 1857, the Christian faith was illegal in Japan. Christians were persecuted — beaten, jailed, many killed. To help identify Christians, the authorities had a number of crucifixes carved in stone and set in the pavement in public places. People were then compelled to step on the cross as they walked past. Those who refused faced the consequences.

My crucifix is a bronze casting made from one of those original stones. It is worn; there is no detail on the figure hanging from the cross, just the outline. It hangs on my wall as a reminder of Christian faithfulness.

One other thought: the wear was caused by the feet which trod on the stone. It is unbelief which scars the body of Christ. The believers, the ones who would not tread there, left no mark, no trace. And, believers or not, they have left no names. We can't honour those who died. But Christ knows and honours them. Luke reports Jesus as saying, "There is nothing hidden which will not be made known" (Luke 12:3). In its context it's a warning to the Pharisees about their hypocrisy, but I think it fair to use it positively too, and say that quiet suffering for Christ may not reach the headlines today, but it is known to Christ, and will be revealed one day. Our discomforts may not compare with martyrdom (although we sometimes act as though they did!) but they are honoured. Luke also records that not even a sparrow is overlooked in God's economy.

Lord, I see the people
walking over your face.
Unconcerned. Laughing.
Just another step on the road of rejection.

I see the figure, worn down.
Sometimes with intent.
More often without thought. Heartbreaking.
Your presence unheeded. Your pain unnoticed.
The ice of indifference burns like flame.
And today,
you are stretched on the cross of my ego.
And the wounds on your body
are from the nails in my shoes.

But there were some, Lord, who held true.
Whose feet led them
to painful glory.
Who can stand in your presence
and meet your eyes.

Lord, I don't know where I'd stand
in that emergency.
On your face, or at your feet?
It's all I can do
to manage the simple courtesies of life.
Living, sharing, helping others.
In your name.
In a crisis, would I stand firm?
I don't know, Lord.
I won't make the brash boasts of Peter,
to follow you everywhere —
until the cock crows.

I just ask for strength, your strength,
and a glimpse of joy.
To get me through today
without too many denials.
And with the wisdom to let tomorrow wait.

And I ask for everyone under pressure today —
keep them near you, Lord.
And guide their feet
into the ways of peace.

Mark 16:1-7

I HAVE just seen the resurrection — or something very like it. A married couple were interviewed at a meeting I attended. Two years ago Doreen was told she had serious cancer. After surgery, the cancer recurred. Last year she was told she'd probably die before Christmas. Her husband, Tom, is a Baptist minister. A year ago the diagnosis was made that he too needed surgery for cancer. They are both still under medical treatment.

It was an honest and moving interview. They'd not found it easy to come to terms with what had happened, with dying, or with not being around any more; or with the thought that one could be left, lonely. But they'd found *today*. Accept today, they said, use it, experience it to the full, enjoy it. Don't worry about the future, today is wonderful. "Spring, this year, has never been so beautiful," said Doreen.

Listening to them, watching them, I suddenly realised that you don't need to die to experience the resurrection. It was there in front of me. In the courage. Of course, they've "died". I guess that in facing the stark realities before them, they've died many deaths. Values and attitudes that seemed important must have changed, or disappeared. But Doreen and Tom were alive, are alive, with a quality of life I can't describe but which I can feel and identify.

Someone has described Christians as people of the resurrection living in a Good Friday world. Tom and Doreen certainly are. I don't know what the future holds for them, and neither do they. In one sense it's important, in another sense it doesn't matter at all, because they've begun to live in the resurrection. Hallelujah! Christ is risen.

Christ is risen. Hallelujah!

It's not always easy, Lord,
to live that statement.
Not always easy to believe,
when it's preached by old men in dark suits,
with faces from which the joy
has long drained away.
Like colour from a well-washed shirt.
Hardly remembered.

Not easy to believe,
living in a Good Friday world.
I can believe in the cross.
The headlines in the paper shout its truth. Everyday.
The suffering. The pain.
Christ mocked and crucified. Afresh.

I stand with Thomas.
Unless I see . . . Handle the evidence.
Find hard-edged proof.
Lord, open my eyes.

I catch a glimmer of the resurrection
like crocus pushing through snow,
purple on white. Still cold.
I see a gleam of life in daffodil gold,
warmer round dark trees.

And suddenly I see the resurrection-splendour
in human courage.
In love.
In the painful, glad acceptance of uncertainty.
The joyous living of today
in the shadow of death.
In lives touched by your hand.
Transformed. Turned triumphantly
to face your light.
The stone rolled away. The tomb empty.
Life ahead, beginning now.

Lord, give me the courage
to reach out
and take it.

Matthew 13:44-46

*C*HRISTIANITY *Rediscovered* is an exciting book. The writer, Vincent Donovan, is a Roman Catholic missionary priest. He writes of his evangelism among the Masai of East Africa. The Masai are a tough, nomadic tribe. I remember visiting some of their kraals in earlier days, travelling in Kenya. They're tall, independent, courageous people. Although not hunters, they'll kill to protect their cattle, and killing a lion with a stabbing spear is still their greatest feat of manhood. (Mine too!)

Donovan, sitting in his mission compound, reading St. Paul's missionary travels, felt compelled to go to the Masai in the way he did. He wouldn't take education, or medicine, or anything else. Except for his faith, he'd go empty-handed, to visit and listen, and to talk about God. His book records the way he was challenged to cut through Western Christian assumptions and make Christ relevant to the Masai through their own lifestyle and culture.

He found problems of language. He describes how, in both Masai and Kiswahili, the word he used for "to believe" really meant "to agree to". One day, a Masai elder told him that the word was ". . . like a hunter shooting an animal with his gun at a distance — only his eyes and fingers took part in the act. For a man really to believe is like a lion going after his prey. His nose and eyes and ears pick up the prey. His legs give him the speed to catch it. All the power of his body is involved in the terrible death leap. . . . And as the animal goes down the lion envelops it in his arms . . . and makes it part of himself. This is the way a lion kills. This is the way a man believes. This is what faith is."

The elder went on. "You told us of the High God, how we must search for him. . . . But we have not done this . . . he has searched us out and found us. All the time we think we are the lion. In the end, the lion is God."

The lion image, like the lion itself, is both beautiful and dangerous. It pictures God's total involvement in seeking us, taking us to himself. It also tells us that faith is God's gift, and that our response can't be a lukewarm agreement from afar, but deep commitment. Like all parables though, don't stretch it too far. The initiative is God's, but we are not his prey. We are his people. "In the end the lion is God." True, but his gift is life, resurrection life. "Lord, increase our faith" (Luke 17:5).

Lord, I stand out in the open,
in the great spaces of your world.
Sometimes it feels good.
My arms stretch, my thoughts expand,
in warm sunshine.

Sometimes it scares me.
The space threatens.
The distances are great
and I don't know what's hiding
behind the next tree.
Am I hunter, or hunted?
What's concealed
in horizon-haze?

It could be you! Looking for me.
Hunting.
Coming closer,
following my footprints.
Relentless in love.

Your love scares me, too.
Because it's two-way.
You love me, Lord. That's fine.
I can go for that.
Comforting,
like cool tree-shade on the veldt.
But your love draws me close. Closer.
Asks for response.
Commitment. Deep down.
That's harder to cope with.
Sometimes, forgive me,
loneliness is easier to bear
than your arms round me.
I can hide from myself in platitudes.
But your love burns them away,
like sun on morning mist,
soon gone.
And in your presence I see my fear,
and know my lack of faith.

Lord, God, Lion of Judah,
help me to understand
that your strength is gentle,
your compulsion courteous.

And that in the light and warmth
of your presence
I am not a victim
but a beloved child.

Lord, strengthen my faith.

Cotswold Landscape

Romans 12:1-12

DURING my time in India I had a pet monkey. Occasionally I gave him a mirror to play with, propping it up on a stone. He would study the reflection, lean towards it, smell it, and then, puzzled, reach his hands around behind the mirror to feel for the other monkey. Another writer describes a baboon with a mirror. This one considered and explored, and then snarled at the reflection, which snarled back. The baboon snarled more menacingly and so did the reflection. This went on until the baboon attacked the mirror and smashed it in his rage, destroying the "danger" which confronted him.

It's a useful picture. Often we project our own anger and fear on to other people, blaming them for what we really are, and saddling them with feelings which are really ours. Feelings, hidden in ourselves, are reflected in other people, and we find it difficult to differentiate between what another person actually feels and what is really a reflection of our own feelings. I can think of interviews I've had to have with "difficult" people. My own anger has kept me on edge and of course the interview has confirmed my own fears. "I knew it would be like that" — but maybe it was my feelings which created the atmosphere and made the other person more aggressive than he need have been. When we are able to stay relaxed and open about such meetings they can be easier, calling out a response in kind.

I think this is echoed in Paul's words to the Christians in Rome (Romans 12:10) ". . . in honour preferring one another . . ." as the Authorised Version says. Paul doesn't ask for doormat humility, allowing everyone to tread on us, but he advocates a respect and restraint in the way we relate to others which calls out the best from both — and which is another way of describing Christian love.

Reaping what we sow is nowhere more true than in our attitudes to others. Often "he got angry with me" means "I acted in such a way that I made him angry with me". Of course we're not always to blame. Sometimes it really is the other person who is aggressive — but we are still free to discern this if we will, and if our sensibility allows us. Then we are free not to respond in kind, but to react with understanding and reassurance. We may not be able to control all the snarls which come our way, but it helps when we understand. Few people are as secure as they appear to be! Take it into account, not to win your argument, but to win their love.

Lord, sometimes the world seems to threaten.
I want to curl up in my corner,
and forget everything. Everybody.
Lock the door, pull the curtains tight.
The action out there is tough,
fast moving.
And when I'm forced into it,
when I have to get involved,
I go into it angry. Aggressive.
Because I'm scared, Lord.
It's not that I want to act that way.
I'd rather be a friend to all.
I'd rather see smiles when I appear,
but, somehow, I'm afraid of my own inadequacy.
And it's because of that, Lord, that I show my teeth,
not in a smile but in a snarl.
To show I'm tough.
To hide the tremor.

Lord, what am I afraid of?
It's not a perfect world, I know.
You know.
You have good cause to know,
remembering the cross.
There's violence and pain.
Doubt and distrust.
And they make people frightened.
Aggressive. Like me.
And underneath, they're trembling. Like me.
Lord, remind me, when I flex my muscles
and clench my fists,
that the only weapon that really guards me
is love.
It's not going to be easy.
The fear, the stress, will still come, do come,
but, Lord, if I'm to win through to peace
it's only through love.
Opening myself to others.
Showing they've nothing to fear from me.
Believing in them,
maybe even before they believe in themselves.
And if I start to love like that
maybe the reflection I'll see in their mirror
will be love too.
Lord, help me start, today.

Matthew 5:38-48

AN article in the *Radio Times* describes two men of violence. One is an alleged leader of the Irish Republican Army, responsible for much bombing and killing in Northern Ireland. The other is a leading "Loyalist", the Protestant backlash, which violently opposes the IRA. The article says:

". . . the two men have many similarities. They are both young, working-class, church-goers, teetotal. Both are affectionate family men. . . ." But it goes on: "Ostensibly nice people, there was a five-per-cent ruthlessness of personality, and when it showed it was frightening. They each had their own justification for killing people. . . ."

How do you react to such a mixed picture? Are they hypocrites, inhuman monsters who hide evil behind a church-going facade? It's hard to couple the respectable attitudes, the family affection, with the killing they both support. It seems so inconsistent.

Yet there's violence in each one of us. Most of us don't go around shooting to kill, bombing, maiming, but we react very strongly when people get in our way. We all have deep feelings of anger just waiting to surface, given half a chance. Violence just under the skin, in spite of our commitment and protestations. We find it hard to come to terms with, and so we press it down deep into our sub-conscious; but it's still there. When it erupts we try to justify it, or blame the other person; so can these men of violence, that's what's so frightening about it. And we are all guilty of violence, in thought and word, if not in deed.

". . . for everyone who hates his brother is a murderer" 1 John 3:15.

It can even be dressed up in religious clothes; as a holy war, defending the faith. The Bible records it: Moses killing an Egyptian overseer; Peter, drawing a sword, and nearly decapitating one of those sent to arrest Jesus.

But when Jesus comes into the picture, the vision changes. He confronts the violence that's in all of us and takes it on himself. By refusing to respond in the same way, by offering love and forgiveness in the face of hate, he breaks the vicious circle of violent response. That's where life and freedom begin; not from the barrel of a gun, not from pride, but from a determined refusal to hate, and an acceptance even of our enemies as people for whom he died. It isn't easy. It wasn't easy for Jesus.

And with Jesus, it's not just a negative "don't be violent" but a positive "love your enemies, do good to them". "Yes, that's great theology," say the cynics, "but you can see it doesn't work in the real world." Some of us would answer, "How do you know? It's never really been tried."

Lord, I long to see your world at peace.
A world where you are in your rightful place.
Where Love Rules, OK?
It would be, if it did.
It seems so far away
your kingdom of peace.
Even further removed from reality
than the holiday brochures at the travel agents.
The stuff of dreams.
Armchair phantasy on a cold Saturday afternoon.
Suddenly shattered by screams of pain.
Exploded by bombs in streets
where the innocent are guilty just by being there.
Where your love is rejected
in wounding bursts of laughter. Rapid fire.

I don't make bombs.
Don't lie in ambush with an Armalite.
But, Lord, it takes so little to pull the pin
that sets me exploding in a shrapnel-burst of hurt ego.
Violence is no stranger.
I may pretend to love.
Adopt the appropriate posture.
But underneath, my thoughts run maverick.
Uncontrolled.

Lord, if I would really see your world at peace,
I need to be at peace myself.
To make a start.
To stand with you in truth
and grasp the anger in my life
and put it in your hands.
To let it go.
And in the empty spaces that it leaves
to feel the inward movement of your love.
Not in the abstract — oh! so easy, Lord,
but in the strong reality of each day.
Let me live today with you.
See others through your eyes.
Live your peace in each particular moment.
One by one.
Not easy, Lord.
But possible. I think.
Lord, hold on tight!

Acts 6:1-7

IF it had been reported in English newspapers today, the headline might have been "Major Row Among Church Leaders", "Racial Discrimination in New Movement", or "Scandal of Hungry Widows!". The more temperate Dr. Luke, recounting the story of the early church, writes "There was disagreement. . . ." His words are less sensational, but honest enough to tell us that things didn't always go smoothly with the first Christians.

Greek-speaking Christians felt they weren't getting fair shares. The apostles were wise: they took the complaint seriously and listened. Then they consulted, talking to everyone. They defined priorities: prayer, preaching, and service. They gave clear responsibilities to particular people so that everyone knew who did what. So far, it sounds like a manual on good management. And the proposals were acceptable to everybody. It worked. It *was* good management.

The story gives us some insight on handling disagreement — what the group-dynamics people call "conflict". The first thing I notice is that disagreement can happen anywhere and everywhere. If it happened in the Spirit-filled church in Jerusalem there's no need to be ashamed when it happens today. The important thing is to handle it the way they did — not to pretend that it doesn't exist, but to bring it out into the open, so that it can be looked at, prayed about, and talked through. (Don't be tempted only to pray about it and shirk the talking!)

The second thing is that disagreement is not necessarily damaging or divisive. It can be, if it's ignored until it builds up into a crisis where everyone is fighting from fixed positions. In this story though, it's dealt with positively, sympathetically, flexibly. There's an evident willingness to change, to listen to the other point of view — a virtue later Christians haven't always had! And a fair solution was found.

Something else intrigues me. It's easy to identify the Holy Spirit motivating the leaders, the whole group, to find agreement and work together. But can we also recognise the same Spirit provoking the initial disagreement? Showing them something was wrong, helping them to grow and develop by the way they tackled it? If we can, it helps us to acknowledge that those we disagree with may be just as well-motivated as we are; not "troublemakers" but fellow builders. Maybe that needs thinking about, but the one thing those early Christians had to have was the ability to face change and respond to new situations.

My last comment is that Luke apparently links this incident with his next observation — in verse 7 — "the word of God spread more and more widely. . . ."

Lord, would you believe me
if I told you that everything's fine?
No tension, no disagreements, no rows.
Sweetness and light.
Life lived in a full gasfired-central-heating-glow
of righteousness and goodwill.
Brotherly love;
not forgetting the sisters.

Not true, Lord.
And, no, you wouldn't believe it anyway.
Your glance takes in the hidden things.
Sees the cracks beneath the paper of piety
I paste over everything.
But I get ashamed, Lord,
that's why I want to hide it all.
The misunderstandings,
the doubts.
Why do I so often suspect the worst of people,
rather than encourage the best?
Manufacture discord. Build walls.
Why is it so much easier
to fold my arms in self defence,
than to open them to another in welcome?

Forgive me, Lord.
And help me see
that whatever my arms are doing
yours are always open.

And when misunderstandings come,
thaw the ice-cold glitter in my eyes
with the spring breeze of your love.
Help me welcome the thoughts of others,
even their criticisms —
that takes some doing, Lord —
as coming from you.

Open my eyes to the wonder of your Spirit
working through them.
It's not always easy to accept, Lord,
but if you can work through me,
with all my problems,
anything's possible.

Gloriously possible!
And, after all,
if you waited for us all to be perfect
before you shared your work with us,
you wouldn't get much done,
would you, Lord?

Old Warsaw Skyline

1 Corinthians 12:12-28

EVER since Desmond Morris wrote *The Naked Ape* and *Manwatching* people have been more aware of body language. I'm unhappy with any view that interprets human actions purely in terms of animal behaviour — there's more to us than that — but it can help our understanding.

Body language describes what each of us communicates, not by what we consciously say or do, but through the signals we make without being aware of them. A simple example: someone being interviewed assures me he's comfortable and happy, but his clenched hands and fidgeting tell me otherwise. I, in my position of power behind the desk, am doing all the talking . . . that's body language.

Someone reminded me the other day about Christians being the body of Christ. A thought struck me. If we are the body of Christ, then there should be a body language which communicates our values and convictions to others — and there is! It's not the things we consciously decide to say and do, but the attitudes we show without being aware of them that communicate our real message. This is true of individuals and of groups. The message varies. There's the natural warm and loving group, welcoming others. There's the cool clique that goes about its own affairs busily, hardly noticing a newcomer. The attitudes can be felt. They say something. The words of love and acceptance we preach can be killed stone-dead if our body language denies them. Consciously or subconsciously, the hearer picks up this other message and sets it alongside our words to see if they match. If they don't, he may not be able to locate the problem, but he'll know something doesn't ring true.

How do we modify the signals? There's the problem. First, by identifying them. Then, not by pretending a new set of attitudes, but only by deepening our commitment to Christ, to love, to people. And certainly not by trying to hide behind the rest of the group. Paul saw that one coming! You can't hide, because the whole body suffers or rejoices with every part.

Lord, it's here again.
The difference between what I say
and what I am.
The words come easy.
I've had a lot of practice with Christian clichés.
The pious phrase,
the shallow patter of unthinking platitudes.
Texts for all seasons.
I hide behind them,
and, with a smile
that goes no further than my face,
I welcome people as I turn away.
Cold shoulder from cool heart.
Preoccupation with my own affairs
that tells others,
in spite of all my words,
that I don't really want to know.
Yes, I'm interested in problems,
just as long as they're mine.

Part of the body of Christ?
Who, me?
Lord, help me to know myself.
To recognize, and face,
just who I am beneath the words.
To open up, to you.
To come out
from behind the choking smokescreen
of spurious spirituality
into the clean air of your truth.
And, in the clear-eyed recognition of who I am,
may I know that I am loved,
and accepted, and healed.
Then, Lord,
I may learn to love and accept,
and share in the healing, of others.
The contradictions will fade,
my words and actions come together.
Not because I can project a new image
of who I am,
but because what people see in me
is you.
And nothing else.

Luke 8:4-8

HAVE you noticed how our reactions to the same thing vary with circumstances? One wintry Saturday morning my wife and I were shopping, slipping and sliding through the snow. It was a nuisance. On Saturday afternoon I went sketching in a local park. Not many people were about, and those who were must have thought me mad, standing ankle deep in snow, poring over a cold sketch pad. But the park was beautiful, the light and shadow, the muted colour, the simplification of form.

For some reason the parable of the sower came to mind. "parable of the snower, more like," I said to myself. Then I thought, "But why not? If Jesus had walked through snowfields instead of through harvest fields wouldn't he have had something to say?" So I took the parable and re-wrote it, in paraphrase anyway. Here it is:

"The snow came. And as it snowed, some snow fell along the footpath, white and pure, until the feet of busy people turned it brown and dirty.

Some snow fell on the road, where it brought peace and silence, until the cars came, skidding and uncontrolled.

Some snow fell on rocky ground, where it remained, white and clean, until the sun came out, and it melted away.

And some snow fell on the mountains, where it gave pleasure to the skier, and joy to all who saw its beauty.

Hear then the parable of the snow. The snow is like the word of God, each flake beautiful and perfect.

The snow on the footpath is like one who hears the word and accepts with joy. But the demands of business and busyness taint and destroy it.

The snow on the road is like one who hears, but the world and its wealth and glamour leads him astray.

The snow on rocky ground is the one who hears and accepts but has no staying power. The thaw comes and his belief is swamped, and flooded, and drowned.

The snow on the mountains is like those who hear, and accept, and their faith becomes a thing of beauty and joy, reaching up to the heavens, declaring the glory of God.

You who have ears to hear, listen to the parable."

So many messages, Lord,
in this world of yours.
Messages that speak your presence,
articulate your care.
Words of love, capsuled in creation.
Alive in the cycle of seasons,
each following each in faithfulness.
In fertile spring.
In pregnant summer promising harvest.
In autumn fulfilment.
The world sings your care.

But the cold wind of winter doubt strikes chill.
Your love falls prodigal on all,
and yet the urgency of busyness chokes my response.
I follow false trails to cul-de-sacs of error.
I'm swept away in faithless flood.
But still your love falls fast on me.
Quietly. Surely.
Drifting round my door in gentle abundance.
Pure. Soft.
Unmeasured and untaxed.
There for the taking.
Enough for all.

Lord, open my eyes
that I may see you in creation power.
Open my heart,
that I may feel your love,
unblocking the arteries of life
to flow without constriction with life-giving warmth.

Open my mind that I may know the glad certainty,
the daily celebration, of your presence.
Not just in nature's revelation,
but in your son.
One with you when life began,
and one with me as it goes on.
Open my lips,
that I may sing your praises
as I walk the road of faith,
today.

Ecclesiastes 3:1-8

AN African field worker in Swaziland was talking to me about his culture. "It's very important," he said, "to take time when you are meeting people; time to make the right greetings, to listen to them, to show respect. If you only have time to rush into a home, put the medicine on the table, and rush out with an apology for being busy, it's better to go at another time when you can be more relaxed." Swazi custom expects you to have time for people, time to listen, time for relationships.

In a different conversation, I heard of a group of nuns in Africa who took a vow not to talk about their faith until someone among the local people first asked them why they had come to work there. The idea may startle some Christians bursting to share their faith, but the more I thought about the idea, the more I understood it. It's more effective talking about your beliefs if they've made your lifestyle sufficiently different for people to notice, and to wonder why. It may take time for this to happen. The pause, the waiting, may then become a time of listening. A time given to us to begin to understand local culture and belief, and people's needs. Then, when we do speak, it's likely to be more relevant, more sympathetic, based on a better understanding, and more acceptable. Too often a quick, aggressive approach can suggest arrogance.

It isn't only Swazi culture that expects people to have time for others. It's widespread. It's only the "efficient", bustling, materialist Western part of the world that hasn't time. We feel time has to be used in doing things and, if we aren't doing things, we feel guilty. Success is measured by actions, not relationships. We make excuses for an abrasive character by saying "Well, he gets things done", when we should be encouraging him to take time to listen to others. There is a time for everything, says the writer in Ecclesiastes, and he includes ". . . a time for silence and a time for speech . . ." (Ecclesiastes 3:7), and I suggest that if these were better balanced in our living we might be more understanding and discerning witnesses.

Time, Lord, time.
I've hardly a moment to think about it!
So much to do,
so much to accomplish.

Lord, slow me down.
Take my foot off the accelerator
and guide it, gently, to the brake.
Cool my overheated mind,
slow my heartbeat.
Tell me again, and again,
that the world,
your world,
will quite possibly survive
without my frantic support.
Remind me that it's not my great endeavour
that keeps the earth's foundations firm.
But yours.

Yet I never sense you in a hurry.
Never feel you don't have the time.
When did Jesus rush around,
shouting "Why aren't there forty-eight hours in a day?"
Like I do.
And he had a lot on his shoulders.
Including a cross.

After all, time is yours.
And eternity.
The world's yours, and its people.
What's that?
Nice of me to admit it?
Lord, when I'm busy,
Dragged down, deep-mired in self-made burdens,
put your hand on my shoulder.
Slow me down.
Help me to see
that people matter more than projects.
That listening and loving mean more
than the endless whirling circles of activity
that dizzy me.
Make me understand
that if I go on rushing around
I'm no different from the rest of my world.

Give me time for people.
Because when I can open the door to them
You'll be able to step in too.

And that's where the difference starts.
And the joy.

Rothorn, Switzerland

Luke 2:25-31

I REMEMBER a Communion Service I shared in, at Salur, in India. It was in a simple, whitewashed room. The bread and wine, under its cloth, were set on an ordinary kitchen table. It was hot. The doors and windows were wide open. Outside were the noises of India. Crows cawing. Heavy trucks, horns blaring, thundering by on the road, threatening mayhem with every screech. Voices raised in the heat, arguing. A powerful loudspeaker on a cycle-rickshaw reminded us that State elections were near. And with this noisy background we repeated the words of Simeon, which we call the Nunc dimitis:

"Lord, now let your servant depart in peace, according to your word; for my eyes have seen your salvation" (Luke 2:29-31).

My thoughts, at the time, concentrated on that last phrase — "my eyes have seen your salvation". Note the tense of the verb — "have seen". Not "will see"; not "hope to see at some time in the dim future". "My eyes *have seen* your salvation."

The Lord's salvation is here and now. In the bread and wine as we knelt to receive it, amid the noise and the dust, and the shouting voices. It has to be part of daily life, experienced now, lived now, shown now. Salvation is gritty. It wasn't achieved by an ethereal spirit walking through the world six inches above the ground to keep his white robes clean. Christ's feet trod where ours tread; in the dust, down where we are. He lived in the noise, tension and dirt of the world. Salvation isn't vacuum-packed, surgically clean. It was achieved in the sweat, tears and blood of the cross.

And it must transform us today. Wherever we are, whatever we do. Each day. It may be covered in the dust of the road, it may be wrapped in pain, it may only be a glimmer of light fighting through cloud but, at the end of today, we pilgrim Christians should be able to join with Simeon and say "we *have seen* your salvation".

There's dust on your feet, Lord.
From the road you walked.
It seems almost disrespectful,
thinking of you like that.
But it's true.
Dirt under your fingernails.
Sweat trickling down your back,
as you walked the rough tracks in Galilee.
Your seamless robe
is spotless in the paintings,
but life says otherwise.
There must have been times
when it smelt of fish, and woodsmoke.

That's good, Lord.
It feels good to know
that you were part, are part, of human living.
That your words, your love
are travelstained.
Born in the turmoil of human relationships,
nurtured in human need.
I thank you,
that salvation comes to me
in flesh and blood.
Gift-wrapped in reality.

Lord, help me live it,
grow my life around it, now.
Help me take the strength I need for today
from the sure knowledge
that salvation surrounds me.

There's dust on your feet, Lord.
That comforts me.
Because when I'm tired,
and vulnerable,
and hurting,
I see you look at me,
and smile.
I hear you say
"I know."
Hallelujah.